GEMS
Of The Spirit

GEMS
Of The Spirit

"Living Activated, Not Aggravated"

Carlos Turner

J. Kenkade
PUBLISHING®
LITTLE ROCK, ARKANSAS

Printed in the United States of America

J. Kenkade Publishing
6104 Forbing Rd
Little Rock, AR 72209
www.jkenkadepublishing.com
Facebook.com/jkenkadepublishing

J. Kenkade Publishing is a registered trademark.

Printed in the United -States of America
ISBN 978-1-944486-83-9

Table of Contents

Dedication

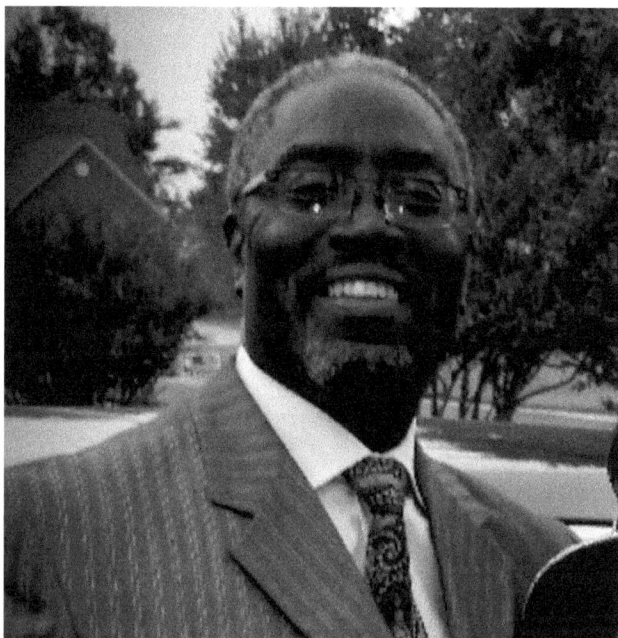

I'm dedicating this book to the late Dr. Lonnie B. Turner. Thank you for sowing the seed in me that pushed me into realms and dimensions I never would've ever imagined. Your desire to see me successful was off the charts, and your love for me as a Nephew was beyond measure. You treated me like I was your own son! I never forgot what you told me at 9 years old. You told me to shoot for the stars, and even if you miss, you will still be amongst the moon. Those words keep me focused on days I want to give up. I love you, I miss you, and until the day of Jesus Christ's return I will continue my journey to make an impact in the Kingdom!

Chapter 1

†

UNDERSTANDING
THE SPIRIT REALM

Before we can even start talking about Gems of the Spirit, you need to know some things about this Realm/Dimension. Both Earth realm and Spirit realm work together to display the desires and plans of God.

What is the Spirit Realm?

Spirit Realm– Is a place where experiences are allowed to be established first with our Words, Thoughts, and Consecration and then exhibited in the earth with our Words, Thoughts, and Consecration.

What most don't understand is everything, whether it's good or bad, starts in the spirit realm. Why? It's because the spirit realm is the mother of all realms. It's the womb and the garden to all things that exist. Words and Thoughts are seeds sown in this realm to create a tangible experience that was once establish in the spirit.

You can't activate the spirit realm (no such thing), but what happens in the spirit realm can activate you! But we can enter into this realm and live in it while we are in the earth.

<u>4 Ways to enter into this realm:</u>
1. Intentional Worship
2. Prayer and Fasting
3. A Prepared Atmosphere
4. Sleep/Dreams

The Bible uses a term that makes reference to the Spirit Realm which is "The Third Heaven"! It is in this realm where we are able to experience Supernatural things that our mind is aware of but hard for our brain to articulate!

In the book of 2 Corinthians 12 Paul shared about an experience he had in this realm! He shared he didn't know if he was in his body or out of his body; however, he was aware that he was caught up in the third heaven (Spirit Realm) and he made contact with a man, which shared revelations so strong it wasn't even lawful for him to share these teachings with nobody else!

I knew a man in Christ above fourteen years ago, (whether in the body, I cannot tell; or whether out of the body, I cannot tell: God knoweth;) such an one caught up to the third heaven. And I knew such a man, (whether in the body, or out of the body, I cannot tell: God knoweth;) How that he was caught up into paradise, and heard unspeakable words, which it is not lawful for a man to utter. 2 Corinthians 12:2-4

Most Bible scholars believe it's making reference to his experience with Jesus on the road of Damascus!

And as he journeyed, he came near Damascus: and suddenly there shined round about him a light from heaven: And he fell to the earth, and heard a voice saying unto him, Saul, Saul, why persecutest thou me? And he said, Who art thou, Lord? And the Lord said, I am Jesus whom thou persecutest: it is hard for thee to kick against the pricks. And he trembling and astonished said, Lord, what wilt thou have me to do? And the Lord said unto him, Arise, and go into the city, and it shall be told thee what thou must do.
Acts 9:3-6

God gives us a picture of how things operate between the Earth Realm and the Spirit Realm as it relates to Angels!

And he dreamed, and behold a ladder set up on the earth, and the top of it reached to heaven: and behold the angels of God ascending and descending on it.
Gen 28:12

I believe that it's safe to say the assignment of Angels is to make divine deliveries, whether it's a message or a blessing, to execute Deliverance and protection for the people of God from negative experiences!

The angel of the LORD encampeth round about them that fear him, and delivereth them.
Psa 34:7

But to which of the angels said he at any time, Sit on my right hand, until I make thine enemies thy footstool?
Heb 1:13

Are they not all ministering spirits, sent forth to minister for them who shall be heirs of salvation?
Heb 1:14

Thank God that we have some Angels working with us and for us in the earth realm! No matter how lonely you may feel, the truth is you are never alone! It's very imperative to know that before we understand anything about Spiritual Warfare! There must be clear understanding about this realm and what you have access to as a believer, especially in times like these!

We have the Power to access stuff in the realm of the spirit and pull the spirit realm experiences into our world! As a matter of fact, Jesus said to pray for it!

And I will give unto thee the keys of the kingdom of heaven: and whatsoever thou shalt bind on earth shall be bound in heaven: and whatsoever thou shalt loose on earth shall be loosed in heaven.
Matt 16:19

After this manner therefore pray ye: Our Father which art in heaven, Hallowed be thy name. Thy kingdom come. Thy will be done in earth, as it is in heaven.
Matt 6:9-10

Hallelujah! Thank God we got Angels and Access!

RHEMA NOTES

_____

_____

_____

_____

_____

_____

_____

_____

_____

_____

_____

_____

_____

_____

_____

_____

Rhema Notes

Rhema Notes

_____
_____
_____
_____
_____
_____
_____
_____
_____
_____
_____
_____
_____
_____
_____
_____
_____
_____
_____
_____
_____
_____
_____
_____
_____
_____
_____
_____

Rhema Notes

RHEMA NOTES

_____

_____

_____

_____

_____

_____

_____

_____

_____

_____

_____

_____

_____

_____

_____

_____

_____

_____

_____

_____

_____

_____

_____

_____

_____

_____

_____

RHEMA NOTES

Chapter 2

✝

WALK IN THE SPIRIT,
LIVE AS A SPIRIT

This I say then, Walk in the Spirit, and ye shall not fulfil the lust of the flesh. Gal 5:16

Before we can address what we need to do in the spirit, we must understand that we are Spirits in a human body having an earthly experience! That's right, you have a Spiritual Body that will last for eternity and a Physical Body (which came from the dust of the earth) that will return back to the dust, from whence it came!

Then shall the dust return to the earth as it was: and the spirit shall return unto God who gave it. Ecc 12:7

Let's look in the book of Genesis so we can discover the origin of our Spiritual Body.

And God said, Let us make man in our image, after our likeness: and let them have dominion over the fish of the sea, and over the fowl of the air, and over the cattle, and over all the earth, and over every creeping thing that creepeth upon the earth. So God created man in his own image, in the image of God created he him; male and female created he them. Gen 1:26-27

So God made us in "his" image! The word Image in Hebrew is **Tseh-lem** which means- "to be in the resemblance of" that means you and I look like God because we came from God! It's the same as with you and your children. Your son or daughter should have some type of features or some type of resemblance of you. If not, something is wrong!

I guess the question at hand is, what does God look like or what is God? Let's examine.

God is a Spirit: and they that worship him must worship him in spirit and in truth. John 4:24

God is in fact is a Spirit, so therefore he looks like a Spirit and because we came from him (the spirit) we are Spiritual beings too! In Gal 5:6 Paul tells the Galatian church to walk in the spirit. The word Walk in the Greek is

Peripateo – it means to conduct or to operate as such!

Why is this important? We must consider that fact like I mentioned in chapter one, the spirit is the mother of all realms. Everything, and I mean everything, starts in the spirit.

So if I am in tune with what's going on in the Spirit, nothing should be able to catch me by surprise in the earth realm. Because walking in the spirit allows me to be proactive instead reactive. It is when I am reactive that the doors to fulfill the lust of the flesh have been opened! The word Lust in the Greek is Epithumuia- it means the craving and desires of the Flesh. So it's safe to say that walking in the spirit helps us to control the cravings of the Flesh!

But in verse 25 he takes it to another level I believe. Let's take a look!

If we live in the Spirit, let us also walk in the Spirit. Gal 5:25

First in verse 24 he gives some good news for those that have received Jesus, like Jesus has crucified the Flesh with the affections and lusts. So after I got my flesh situation under control, he connects two statements together. He said, "If we live in the spirit, let us walk in the spirit! The word Live in the Greek is **Zao**- it means to be powerful, strong, and to breathe. So in Gen 2:7 what did God do for man?

Let's take a look.

And the LORD God formed man of the dust of the ground, and breathed into his nostrils the breath of life; and man became a living soul. Gen 2:7

He breathed into man's nostrils and man became a living being! I believe as believers as we walk in the Spirit and because we are spirits of God, God has given us the power and the capacity to breathe life into the lives of those that just exist but don't have life! We have to power speak life into every dead area of people lives and command all dry bones to live in Jesus name!

The hand of the LORD was upon me, and carried me out in the spirit of the LORD, and set me down in the midst of the valley which was full of bones, And caused me to pass by them round about: and, behold, there were very many in the open valley; and, lo, they were very dry. And he said unto me, Son of man, can these bones live? And I answered, O Lord GOD, thou knowest. Again he said unto me, Prophesy upon these bones, and say unto them, O ye dry bones, hear the word of the LORD. Thus saith the Lord GOD unto these bones; Behold, I will cause breath to enter into you, and ye shall live: And I will lay sinews upon you, and will bring up flesh upon you, and cover you with skin, and put breath in you, and ye shall live; and ye shall know that I am the LORD. So I prophesied as I was commanded: and as I prophesied, there was a noise, and behold a shaking, and the bones came together, bone to his bone. And when I beheld, lo, the sinews and the flesh came up upon them, and the skin covered them above: but there was no breath in them. Then said he unto me, Prophesy unto the wind, prophesy, son of man, and say to the wind, Thus saith the Lord GOD; Come from the four winds, O breath, and breathe upon these slain, that they may live. Eze 37:1-9

Don't stay comfortable walking in the spirit. Take your place in the spirit and live in the spirit. You are anointed to resuscitate those that have lost their breath in this life. Help somebody breathe again!

RHEMA NOTES

_____

_____

_____

_____

_____

_____

_____

_____

_____

_____

_____

_____

_____

_____

_____

_____

_____

_____

RHEMA NOTES

_____
_____
_____
_____
_____
_____
_____
_____
_____
_____
_____
_____
_____
_____
_____
_____
_____
_____
_____
_____
_____
_____
_____
_____
_____
_____
_____
_____
_____
_____

Rhema Notes

Rhema Notes

Rhema Notes

Rhema Notes

Chapter 3

✝

SPIRITUAL GIFTS

Wanting to be used by God and operate in spiritual gifts is a wonderful thing, but what's more important is that you know the function of what you are trying to operate in.

Lack of knowledge can be destructive, and what is meant to bless others without the proper teaching will hurt many!

My people are destroyed for lack of knowledge:
because thou hast rejected knowledge, I will also reject
thee, that thou shalt be no priest to me. Hos 4:6

Good intention works well in the natural realm, but in the spirit you have to be very careful because you are dealing with forces that are not of this world.

Spiritual Gifts are supernatural endowments, not necessary talents and abilities. These gifts operate through the Holy Ghost with Power!

But ye shall receive power, after that the Holy Ghost is come upon you. Acts 1:8

Jesus promises us that what he has done we will do too and even far greater.

Verily, verily, I say unto you, He that believeth on me, the works that I do shall he do also; and greater works than these shall he do; because I go unto my Father. John 14:12

God wants you to flow and operate in spiritual gifts, you just need the wisdom to do so along with the anointing!

Now concerning spiritual gifts, brethren, I would not have you ignorant. 1 Cor 12:1

Let's dive into this!

Now there are diversities of gifts, but the same Spirit. And there are differences of administrations, but the same Lord. And there are diversities of operations, but it is the same God which worketh all in all. But the manifestation of the Spirit is given to every man to profit withal. For to one is given by the Spirit the word of wisdom; to another the word of knowledge by the same Spirit; To another faith by the same Spirit; to another the gifts of healing by the same Spirit; To another the working of miracles; to another prophecy; to another discerning of spirits; to another divers kinds of tongues; to another the interpretation of tongues: But all these worketh that one and the selfsame Spirit, dividing to every man severally as he will. 1 Cor 12:4-11

So we can see we have nine spiritual gifts that Paul is talking about. Hopefully when this chapter is over you will have a clear understanding on this subject.

First allow me to put the gifts in categories because they all have different functions, but some are in the same category.

There are 3 Categories:

The Revelation Category:
The Gifts of Revelation– Reveal something
The Power Category:
The Gifts of Power– Do something
The Utterance Category:
The Gifts of Utterance– Say something

The Revelation Cateory has 3 gifts under its umbrella. The Gift of Knowledge, Wisdom, and Discerning of Spirits.

The First one we are going to deal with is the gift of Knowledge.

Knowledge- the Greek root word is ***Ginosko,*** which means to be aware of, perceive, or to understand.

The Gift of Knowledge – A supernatural revelation of God's will; divine insight concerning circumstances and situations that are happening or have happened. Because of the power of Revelation, it often gets mistaken for Prophesy because of its accuracy of the unknown.

The Second one is the gift of Wisdom.

Wisdom comes from the Greek word ***Sophia,*** which simply means wisdom.

The Gift of Wisdom – A Spiritual capacity and enablement that allows a person to bring application from the knowledge of God's will. People that have this powerful gift know what to do and when to do it in any given season.

The Third one is the Discerning of Spirits.

Discerning- the root word is ***Diakrino,*** which means to separate, oppose, and judge.

Spirits- the Greek word is ***Pueuma,*** meaning breath or breeze

The Gift of Discerning of Spirits – A gift that allows one to detect spiritual, supernatural powers that are at work in a person, place, or thing.

This is in fact a powerful gift! The kingdom of darkness hates people that have this gift because they can see what others can't!

Let's move on to the next category.
We've got a lot to cover!

The next category is the Power Category: Remember the Power Gifts "DO" something!

The Power Category includes The Gift of Faith, Working of Miracles, and The Gift of Healing. Let's get into it!

The First gift is the gift of Faith.

Faith- the Greek word is *Pistis*- it implies truth, assurance, and conviction

The Gift of Faith– is a supernatural ability to trust God and expect results.

This is not normal faith. This gift gives believers access into realms that make things happen in the earth realm.

The Second gift is the gift of Miracles.

Miracles- the Greek word is *Dunamis*, implying Miraculous Power, abilities, and might

The Gift of Miracles– it is an intervention of God in the course of nature that demonstrates his power.

This gift has the capacity to shift the paradigm of non-believers. Many souls have been saved by witnessing the Power of God through the gift of miracles.

The Third gift is the gift of Healing.

Healing- the Greek word is *Iaomai*- it means to cure and heal.

The Gift of Healing– is the manifestation of God's power to cure and heal physical and/or emotional sickness without the aid of a human.

The next category is the gifts of Utterance Category: Remember the Utterance Gifts "Say" something!

The Utterance Category includes Divers kinds of tongues, the Interpretation of Tongues, and The Gift of Prophecy.

The first gift is the gift of Divers kinds of tongues.

Tongues- the root word is *Glossa*, which means a language that's not acquired naturally!

Gift of Tongues– a spiritual language that's holy from a believer that might or might not be understood by the speaker

The person that has this gift allows the Holy Ghost to use them to speak languages that can only come from the spirit.

The second gift is the Interpretation of Tongues.

Interpretation- the Greek word is *Hermenia*- it means Translation.

Interpretation of Tongues– a supernatural ability to comprehend what's been said in order to edify the church or a group of people

Those with this gift cannot be so easily distracted by life circumstances. They must be in tune at all times in order to translate the will of God to any group of people.

The third gift, but not least, is the Gift of Prophecy.

Prophecy- the Greek word is *Prophetes*, which

means an inspired speaker, poet, or foreteller.

The Gift of Prophecy– having a God-inspired procla-
mation to build, instruct, foretell, and comfort

Allow me to say this, Spiritual Gifts manifest differ-
ently according to the amount of grace given for that area.

*But unto every one of us is given grace according
to the measure of the gift of Christ. Eph 4:7*

How do we increase Grace?

*But he giveth more grace. Wherefore he saith,
God resisteth the proud, but giveth grace unto
the humble. Jam 4:6*

Let me say this for those of you that may feel like you
don't qualify. Even if you weren't born with it, with the
proper training and understanding you can still have
it. Yes, that's right! Especially if it's desired out of love!

*Follow after charity, and desire
spiritualgifts. 1 Cor 14:1*

So the question is, what's needed from
me to activate the spiritual gifts in my life?

1. Faith *(Rom 12:6)*
*Having then gifts differing according to the
grace that is given to us, whether prophecy, let
us prophesy according to the proportion of faith;*

2. Knowledge *(Prov 8:9)*
They are all plain to him that understandeth, and right to them that find knowledge.

3. Grace *(Luke 2:40)*
And the child grew, and waxed strong in spirit, filled with wisdom: and the grace of God was upon him.

4. Desire *(Mark 11:24)*
Therefore I say unto you, What things soever ye desire, when ye pray, believe that ye receive them, and ye shall have them.

Seek the father, spend time in prayer with fasting, position yourself, and walk in Holiness and you too will be used by God in the gifts of the spirit. Don't procrastinate because the kingdom of God needs you!

RHEMA NOTES

Rhema Notes

Rhema Notes

RHEMA NOTES

Rhema Notes

Rhema Notes

Rhema Notes

Chapter 4

✝

UNDERSTANDING SPIRITUAL WARS AND CONFLICTS

For the weapons of our warfare are not carnal, but mighty through God to the pulling down of strong holds; Casting down imaginations, and every high thing that exalteth itself against the knowledge of God, and bringing into captivity every thought to the obedience of Christ. 2 Cor.10:4-5

Warfare- the Greek word is *stra'teia*– it's when a Military unit, company, or nation (people) experience conflict in an assignment that's been put in motion.

Warfare ain't Warfare unless you are fighting with a Unit or for a Unit because of the assignment that's given.

What are our Weapons?

It's NOT TONGUES..... most people think the gift of tongues is a weapon, this is not true. However, it is a tool of the Holy Ghost that gives you the power to do whatever is necessary in the spirit realm.

Let's consider what tongues do:

1. *Edify you*– 1 Cor 14:2-14 (this is why folks don't know what's happening in the spirit)

For he that speaketh in an unknown tongue speaketh not unto men, but unto God: for no man understandeth him; howbeit in the spirit he speaketh mysteries. But he that prophesieth speaketh unto men to edification, and exhortation, and comfort. He that speaketh in an unknown tongue edifieth himself; but he that prophesieth edifieth the church. I would that ye all spake with tongues, but rather that ye prophesied: for greater is he that prophesieth than he that speaketh with tongues, except he interpret, that the church may receive edifying. Now, brethren, if I come unto you speaking with tongues, what shall I profit you, except I shall speak to you either by revelation, or by knowledge, or by prophesying, or by doctrine? And even things without life giving sound, whether pipe or harp, except they give a distinction in the sounds, how shall it be known what is piped or harped? For if the trumpet give an uncertain sound, who shall prepare himself to the battle? So likewise ye, except ye utter by the tongue words easy to be understood, how shall it be known what is spoken? for

ye shall speak into the air. There are, it may be, so many kinds of voices in the world, and none of them is without signification. Therefore if I know not the meaning of the voice, I shall be unto him that speaketh a barbarian, and he that speaketh shall be a barbarian unto me. Even so ye, forasmuch as ye are zealous of spiritual gifts, seek that ye may excel to the edifying of the church. Wherefore let him that speaketh in an unknown tongue pray that he may interpret. For if I pray in an unknown tongue, my spirit prayeth, but my understanding is unfruitful.
1 Cor 14:2-14

2. *It's sign you have the Holy Ghost-* Acts 2:4

And they were all filled with the Holy Ghost, and began to speak with other tongues, as the Spirit gave them utterance. Acts 2:4

So it's safe to say that tongues is the evidence that we have the "POWER" to engage in Warfare but it's not a weapon itself! Demons are not moved by your spiritual language (why) because they know spiritual languages too!

But ye shall receive power, after that the Holy Ghost is come upon you: and ye shall be witnesses unto me both in Jerusalem, and in all Judaea, and in Samaria, and unto the uttermost part of the earth. Acts 1:8

But our weapons are MIGHTY through God!

Who was Mighty through God?– JESUS!
So our weapons come through Jesus (Not Carnal)
Let's examine what's mighty through Jesus!

1. The Name of Jesus– Phil 2:10
2. Mind of Jesus (Spiritual Thinking)– Phil 2:5
3. Strips of Jesus (Healing)– Isa 53:5
4. Blood of Jesus (Access to God and the things of God)– Heb 10:19
5. DBR (Death, Burial, and Resurrection) of Jesus (Salvation/Eternal Life)– John 11:25
6. Ghost of Jesus (For "Power")– Acts 1:8

These are the 6 things that pull down STRONG-HOLDS!!!

Glory to the Lamb of God that liveth forever! Hallelujah!

Let's dig deeper!

So the question is: Are we being tested, are we wrestling, or in Warfare? Let's examine because everything ain't warfare!

Take a look at 1 Peter 1:7

That the trial of your faith, being much more precious than of gold that perisheth, though it be tried with fire, might be found unto praise and honour and glory at the appearing of Jesus Christ. 1 Pet 1:7

Trial- it comes from the Greek word ***dokimion*** which means to be proved via a test.

*Test?– What's being tested? "My Faith is being tested and James 1:3 tells us why.

Knowing this, that the trying of your faith worketh patience. Jam 1:3

So it's safe to say sometimes being tested may feel like warfare because the test itself assignment is to strengthen my faith, but it's taking "Patience" to do it. This in some ways convinces my soul (My Will, My Mind, My Emotions) that this must be a warfare when in fact it's only a test! Now let's take a deeper look into Wrestling.

And Jacob was left alone; and there wrestled a man with him until the breaking of the day. And when he saw that he prevailed not against him, he touched the hollow of his thigh; and the hollow of Jacob's thigh was out of joint, as he wrestled with him. And he said, Let me go, for the day breaketh. And he said, I will not let thee go, except thou bless me. And he said unto him, What is thy name? And he said, Jacob. And he said, Thy name shall be called no more Jacob, but Israel: for as a prince hast thou power with God and with men, and hast prevailed. And Jacob asked him, and said, Tell me, I pray thee, thy name. And he said, Wherefore is it that thou dost ask after my name? And he blessed him there. Gen 32: 24-29

Wrestle in Hebrew is *abaq* it literally means to get dusty or dirty.

*So what is Wrestling? I am of the persuasion that wrestling was a method of "Character and Integrity Building".

While wrestling with the Angel, Jacob experienced a shift in his Character and Integrity!

The Hebrew word "Abaq" for wrestling means to get dusty. I believe this wrestling match was to show Jacob just how dusty and dirty he really was. Being the trickster that he was he needed that match to see himself. That led to his transformation! Sometimes God allows things to come into our lives to correct our Character and Integrity because our flesh and mindset don't want to shift. It becomes a Wrestling match when God is ready to change our Paradigm!

So as we can see, everything we go through in life is not Warfare. God is working either on our Faith, Patience, Character and Integrity! You are being conformed, shaped, and molded into the image of his son Jesus!

For whom he did foreknow, he also did predestinate to be conformed to the image of his Son, that he might be the firstborn among many brethren. Rom 8:29

Testing and Wrestling become necessary when a transformation and elevation is required!

Rhema Notes

Rhema Notes

Rhema Notes

_____

_____

_____

_____

_____

_____

_____

_____

_____

_____

_____

_____

_____

_____

_____

_____

_____

_____

_____

_____

_____

_____

_____

_____

_____

_____

_____

_____

Rhema Notes

RHEMA NOTES

_____

_____

_____

_____

_____

_____

_____

_____

_____

_____

_____

_____

_____

_____

_____

_____

_____

_____

_____

_____

_____

_____

_____

_____

_____

_____

_____

_____

_____

_____

Rhema Notes

Chapter 5

✝

Don't License your Spiritual Enemy

Neither give place to the devil. Eph 4:27

Place (*to'pos*)– Privilege to do, or a License The birth of a person's warfare is in the AREA or TERRITORY you refused to grant a License for! **If you have given him a license, there's no need for WARFARE!** But because you have decided to MANAGE and MAINTAIN your territory, you just initiated a FIGHT!

So shall they fear the name of the LORD from the west, and his glory from the rising of the sun. When the enemy shall come in like a flood, the Spirit of the LORD shall lift up a standard against him. Isa 59:19

He'll try to force his way in!

5 Major Licenses of Life:

Assignment License—What you were created to do to please God

Mental License—The controlling capacity of how you think, because thinking creates!

Financial License— Your currency and money flow that connects and controls impact

Health License—Your physical body or you as a vessel (Broken vessels leak!)

Happiness License— Relationships and things that brings wholeness into your life

When a license has been granted to the kingdom of darkness, the gates of hell are opened!

"Understanding The Gates of Hell"

And Jesus answered and said unto him, Blessed art thou, Simon Barjona: for flesh and blood hath not revealed it unto thee, but my Father which is in heaven. And I say also unto thee, That thou art Peter, and upon this rock I will build my church; and the gates of hell shall not prevail against it. And I will give unto thee the keys of the kingdom of heaven: and whatsoever thou shalt bind on earth shall be bound in heaven: and whatsoever thou shalt loose on earth shall be loosed in heaven. Matt 16:17-19

Let's look at the Gates of Hell
Gates = (*poo'lay*)– Opening, portals, exits, or operations
That addresses you Personally!

For we wrestle not against flesh and blood, but against principalities, against powers, against the rulers of the darkness of this world, against spiritual wickedness in high places. Eph. 6:12

Wrestle (*Pa'lay*)– a contest between 2 parties that intends to throw one down and to hold one down with his hand by the neck. (Why?)
To apply a Yoke around the neck to limit 3 things: Sight, Direction, and Mobility

Principalities– (**arch o mai**) = "Hindering Spirits" *1st in Rank
Powers– (**exou'sia**) = "Manipulating Spirits" *Delegated Authority
Rulers of Darkness– (**sko'tos**) = "Controlling Spirits" *Officers of Blindness
Spiritual Wickedness– (**p'neu'ma'tikos**) "Destructive Spirits" * Lofty place of the Mind
These four departments keep you blind to your Divine Nature! But you have Power and authority over all the Powers of the enemy! Glory to God!

Then he called his twelve disciples together, and gave them power and authority over all devils, and to cure diseases. Luke 9:1

According as his divine power hath given unto us all things that pertain unto life and godliness, through the knowledge of him that hath called us to glory and virtue: Whereby are given unto us exceeding great and precious promises: that by these ye might be partakers of the divine nature, having escaped the corruption that is in the world through lust. 2 Pet 1:3-4

**When you wake up your Divine Nature,
you learn to see past the Natural!!!**

Here are 6 areas in which demonic spirits are always at work to hinder you from operating in your Divine Nature:

1. Mind– How we need to think
2. Mouth– What we declare
3. Ministry– What and who we are supposed to serve
4. Mission– What we are supposed to be doing
5. Metron– Our effectiveness in the measure or the sphere of influence given to us
6. Manifestation– What belongs to us for the assignment

If there's no understanding or drive to function accurately in these spheres, the enemy will start to replace these areas with demonic Misery!!!

GEMS *Of The Spirit*

The enemy knows once you learn how to think- (Mind)

Know what to declare- (Mouth)

Know what and who you are supposed to serve- (Ministry)

Know what you are supposed to be doing- (Mission)

Know how to be effective in your sphere of influence- (Metron)

Know what belongs to you for the assignment- (Manifestation)

YOU ARE GOING TO BE UNSTOPPABLE!!!
Take your License back, give no place to the devil!

RHEMA NOTES

_____
_____
_____
_____
_____
_____
_____
_____
_____
_____
_____
_____
_____
_____
_____
_____
_____

RHEMA NOTES

Rhema Notes

Rhema Notes

Rhema Notes

Rhema Notes

Chapter 6

✝

Voices, Did I Just Hear That?

Did I just hear that? This is a question we often ask ourselves. The problem is we don't know where the Voice is even coming from. There's no one around and either internally or externally you hear a statement or a command and wonder to yourself: Who said that, and why? Let's consider the word as we address the sphere of spiritual Voices.

There are, it may be, so many kinds of voices in the world, and none of them is without signification. Therefore if I know not the meaning of the voice, I shall be unto him that speaketh barbarian, and he that speaketh shall be a barbarian unto me. 1 Cor 14:10-11

The Word Voices comes from the Greek word *phone*, which means a certain sound, noise, tone, or even a language.

It is this Greek word Phone where we get the word Tele-Phone from. The prefix "Tele" actually means from a distance, so a telephone is a device we use to exchange sound, tone, noise, and languages from a distance.

But in the spirit realm, what if I can't recognize the sound or the language? In the natural we hang up, don't we? But in the spirit voices will continue until you acknowledge them, pay some attention, or react.

Let's take a deeper look, Paul said there are so many kinds of Voices in the world, and none of them is without signification.

Now the word Signification in the Greek is *aphonos*, that means with a purpose, for a reason, and a sign.

So it's safe to say all voices that are heard have a meaning, reason, a purpose, and an agenda! So it's important that we know who or what is talking at that time.

Allow me to give you a few nuggets about voices and the impact they can have on your life.

1. The VOICE you obey is the one you are a servant to.

2. The VOICE you obey will determine either your funeral or future.

3. VOICES are seeds/sperm to all decisions.

4. What VOICE you choose to listen to will promote you or prostitute you.

As you can see, what and who you listen to can have a major impact on your life, destiny, and future. Paul said there are so many kinds of voices in the world, so we are going to delve into the 3 major voices that operate in the world from the spirit realm. Let's see who's talking!

There are 3 Major Voices that operate in the world:
1. The Adamic (Adam) Voice
2. The Satanic Voice
3. The Voice of God

Let's deal with the voice that most are familiar with, and that is the Adamic voice (Your Own Voice).

***The Adamic Voice*-** is self-motivating and promoting. How you know it's you is because you are pushed by your own ambitions and drive. It's when you do something without God's instruction and direction. The reason for this is because ambition talks to you daily and keeps you positive, and that's good to help you to maneuver through certain seasons in your life, but when it's time to make a major move, you need to hear from the Creator in order to know what to do. (Read 1 Chron 13:9-13; 1 Chron 15:1-2, 13)

Also, when the Adamic voice is speaking in your head one thing to notice is it's always motivated by good ideas but not necessarily God ideas. The Adamic voice thrives off of the mood or the emotional state of a person. So the Adamic voice will force you to rush because your feeling is sending signal that God is taking too long. And guess what, you will start to listen more to yourself. Has anybody been there before? (Read Gen 16:1-2, 4, 15-16; Gen 17:19; Gen 21:2-3, 8-9, 12-13)

The second Voice we are going to deal with is the Satanic Voice.

The Satanic Voice – This voice is used through 4 different channels.

1. Familiar Spirits
2. Demons
3. Falling Angels
4. The Devil himself

I want to give you 4 things to consider so you can determine whether or not the voice you are hearing is of God.

1. This voice will cause a believer to do something the father never told nor confirmed for them to do. See 1 Chron. 21:1, 7-13

2. This voice will force you to choose what looks good to you but is not good for you. See Matt 4:8-10

3. This voice makes propositions that are in harmony with your struggle of appetite. See Gen 3:3-6

4. This voice speaks or releases ideas that war against your divine mission or purpose in life. See Matt 16:21-24

The third Voice is the most important voice, this is the Voice of the Holy Spirit or the Voice of God himself!

The Voice of God– the Voice of God is channeled through the Holy Spirit.

If you are believer and have a relationship with God, the more time you spend with him in meditation and prayer you will learn his voice. Knowing his voice is proof that you belong to him! Let's take a look in the Word.

And when he putteth forth his own sheep, he goeth before them, and the sheep follow him: for they know his voice. And a stranger will they not follow, but will flee from him: for they know not the voice of strangers. John 10:4-5

My sheep hear my voice, and I know them, and they follow me. John 10:27

Let's take a look in verse 27: Jesus said, sheep hear my voice, but in verse 4 he gave the parable about how sheep should know the Shepard's voice. This is a clear distinction between hearing and knowing. When you are introduced to Christ, you hear his voice.

While it is said, Today if ye will hear his voice, harden not your hearts, as in the provocation. Heb 3:15

But as you mature in the things of God you will begin to know the voice and keep yourself in position to be obedient!

So the question is: How and when does the Holy Spirit speak to us on behalf of God himself?

Let's consider the Gospel according to John:

But the Comforter, which is the Holy Ghost, whom the Father will send in my name, he shall teach you all things, and bring all things to your remembrance, whatsoever I have said unto you. John 14:26

In order for the Holy Spirit, the parakletos, to do what Jesus said he was supposed to do, he has to have a Voice in order to do these things. So YES, the Holy Spirit talks and speaks on behalf of God.

Let's take a look. The first assignment of the Holy Spirit is he is going to Teach. That word in the Greek is did'asko, which means to instruct, to order in the direction of. Well you can't teach without a voice, so the Holy Ghost has a voice in order to teach us.

The second assignment of the Holy Spirit is to Remind. That word in the Greek is **hupomimnesko**, which means to bring up quietly, to put it in the mind. Guess what? A voice is needed in order to bring something up quietly. It's not the volume of the voice that's important but it's the value of the words coming from it!

Voices are powerful tools for the Kingdom of God and the Kingdom of Darkness. Ask the father for the gift of discernment to know the difference between them all.

✝

The Conclusion

There's such a hunger for the things of the spirit and the supernatural. Many have decided to tap into the dark side in order to understand more about the Supernatural and the things of the spirit. One of the reasons for this, I believe, is because the church as a whole has lost the desire to see a move of God validated by his power with miracles, signs, and wonders. It's my desire and prayer that this information will activate you in ways you never dreamed as you apply it to your spiritual life. I bless you my brothers and sisters!

May the Lord bless thee, may the Lord keep thee, may the Lord lift up his countenance on thee and give thee peace! May you discover more things in God as you maneuver in the things of the spirit. Shalom and Amen!

Rhema Notes

_____
_____
_____
_____

_____
_____
_____
_____
_____
_____
_____
_____
_____
_____
_____
_____
_____
_____
_____
_____
_____
_____
_____
_____
_____
_____
_____
_____

Rhema Notes

Rhema Notes

Rhema Notes

Rhema Notes

Rhema Notes

RHEMA NOTES

ABOUT THE AUTHOR

APOSTLE C. A. TURNER is the prophetic voice for this last hour. He is the Senior Pastor and Founder of Kingdom Nation Ministries and About Gods Business World Outreach ministries in Jonesboro, AR and Memphis, TN. He has been preaching and teaching for over 25 years, reaching the lost at all cost and impacting the earth with the things concerning the kingdom of God with miracles, signs, and wonders operating within his ministry. He attended Grambling State University with a focus in Business Administration. He also Attended the School of Exodus studying Theology and Biblical Studies. He is the founder of Y.E.S.S. Young Entrepreneur Success School for the urban youth with a focus in financial Literacy. Carlos Turner is the owner and CEO of several successful businesses, Kingdom Clean Detailing, Tojoe's Wings and Waffles, Turner and Thomas Real Estate, Carlo Avery Fashions, and Olive Tree Finance and Investment Firm. In his spare time, he loves reading, studying, and researching the things of the spirit to stay sharp and alert for the things to come! His favorite verse is found in the book of Luke 1:37 that says, "For with God nothing shall be impossible!" His assignment is to shake and reawaken the body of Christ in the area of the supernatural. He understands that this will be a life journey, so he is totally committed to the things of God and strictly being about God's Business.

J. Kenkade
PUBLISHING ®

Our Motto
"Transforming Life Stories"

Publish Your Book With Us

Our All-Inclusive Self-Publishing Packages

100% Royalties
Professional Proofreading & Editing
Interior Design & Cover Design
Self-Publishing Tutorial & More

For Manuscript Submission or other inquiries:
www.jkenkadepublishing.com
(501) 482-JKEN

Also Available from this Author

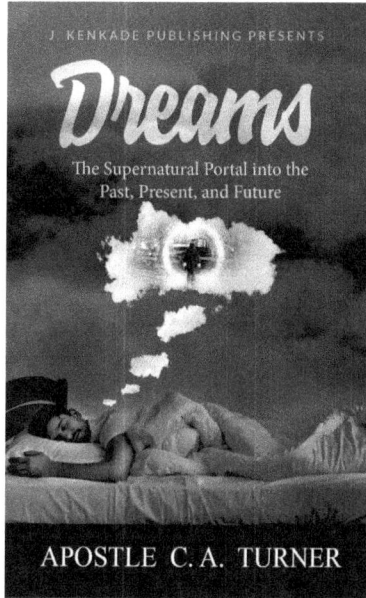

ISBN: 978-1-944486-78-5
Visit www.amazon.com
Author: Apostle C. A. Turner

A study on the supernatural realm of Dreams, how God speaks to us in our sleep, and what scripture has to say on this matter.

Also Available from
J. Kenkade Publishing

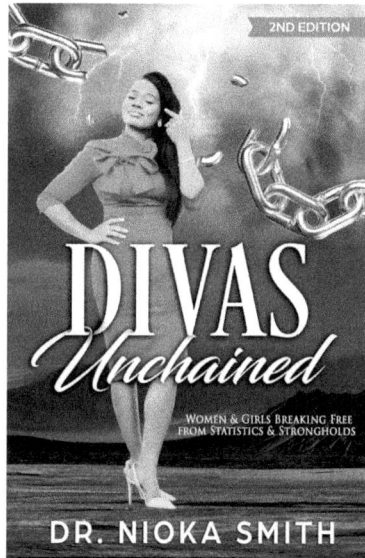

ISBN: 978-1-944486-25-9
Visit www.drniokasmith.com
Author: Dr. Nioka Smith

Sexually abused by her father at the age of 14, pregnant at the age of 17, and a nervous breakdown at the age of 28, Dr. Nioka Smith's painful past almost killed her, until the voice of the Lord guided her into destroying strongholds and reversing Satan's plan for her life. DIVAS Unchained is the powerful chain-breaking reality of the many unfortunate strongholds our women and girls face. Dr. Nioka uses her divine gift to help women and girls break free from destructive life cycles and prosper in all areas of life. Satan has lied to you. It's time to expose his lies. It's time to break free!

Also Available from
J. Kenkade Publishing

ISBN: 978-1-944486-73-0
Visit www.amazon.com
Author: Jerry Walker

Life shouldn't be happening to us; we should be happening to life. This is what living in excellence is all about: Using every talent, gift, capacity and revelation that God has equipped us with and reaching our fullest potential. In this 31-Day guide, you will discover how meditating and reflecting on the word of God can pull you into His divine plan for your life. Prepare to expand past mediocrity and live a life of excellence!

Also Available from
J. Kenkade Publishing

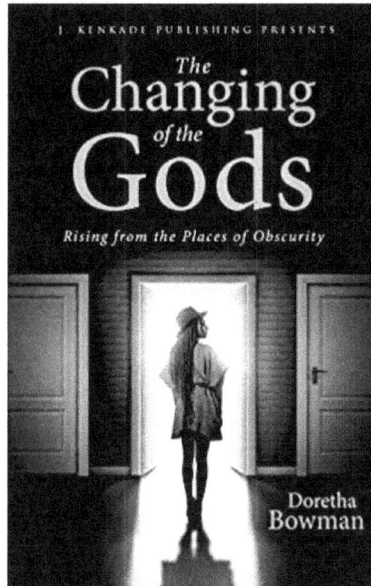

ISBN: 978-1-944486-26-6
Visit www.amazon.com
Author: Doretha Bowman

"The Changing of the Gods" describes one woman's life as it clung to the blind idolization of sin. From drug abuse, alcoholism, and victimization of sexual abuse, Doretha finds a way to make peace with her past through the aid of the guiding light of Christ, the true God. This book allows readers to acknowledge and rise from their places of obscurity to finally find the areas of their life that can be transformed by the light of Jesus Christ's salvation.

Also Available from
J. Kenkade Publishing

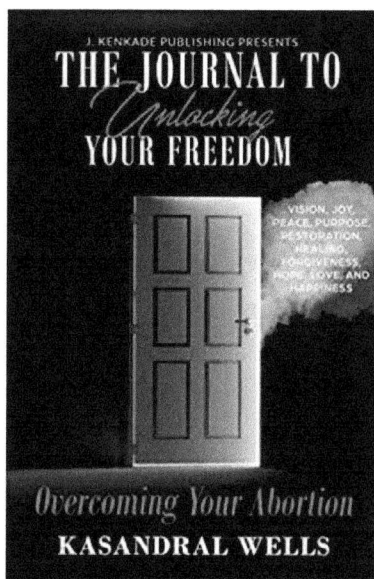

ISBN: 978-1-944486-56-3
Visit www.amazon.com
Author: Kasandral Wells

This is a therapeutic journal with writing prompts and scripture to help anyone process their emotions and experience after having an abortion.

www.ingramcontent.com/pod-product-compliance
Lightning Source LLC
LaVergne TN
LVHW051813080426
835513LV00017B/1939